Partly Cloudy

gary soto

Partly Cloudy

Poems of Love and Longing

Harcourt

Houghton Mifflin Harcourt

Boston   New York   2009

Harcourt is an imprint of Houghton Mifflin Harcourt Publishing
Company.

www.hmhbooks.com

Text set in Berling
Designed by Linda Lockowitz

Library of Congress Cataloging-in-Publication Data
Soto, Gary.
Partly cloudy: poems of love and longing/Gary Soto.
p.   cm.
1. Teenagers—Poetry.   2. First loves—Poetry.   3. Love poetry,
American.   4. Young adult poetry, American.   I. Title.
PS3569.O72P37   2009
811'.54—dc22   2008022267
ISBN 978-0-15-206301-6

Printed in the United States of America
H G F E D C B A

To Isabel Schon
It's 40–Love, and your serve

Contents

A Girl's Tears, Her Songs

A Boy's Body, His Words

A Girl's Tears,
Her Songs

On the Side of a Bike Path

What was our future? I turned over
Your hand and studied your palm.
I noted two lines, one short, the other long.
I looked at mine—three lines,
One filled with sweat from our three-mile ride.
I wondered to myself, *Why three?*
Then I knew—you were the first
To lie with me on a blanket,
And two others would follow,
Neither as beautiful.
As you stood up,
Shaking grass from your hair,
I gripped your hand—pinched it, really.
Months from now you will not be mine.

Not Yet

The weakest petals
Blow from the flowering tree,
And I think of myself
As a part of that tree,
My petals intact.
Not yet, I tell you,
We're young, just
Coming into bloom,
Our roots sinking
Daily into the earth.
Not yet, I tell you,
I a small tree,
You a taller, bending
Tree. The sun
Will roll over us,
And if a cloud
Of worry throws lightning,
Let's remember our fear.

Composition

Cold day, cold without you,
Ice hanging from the eaves like teeth
And the sun riding out of town before I changed
Out of my pajamas. To get warm, I opened a can
Of alphabet soup, got it boiling,
And poured it into a bowl. The bowl was warm
As your hand. I liked that, steam curling
As I carefully carried it to the table.
I drank from the lip of the bowl,
And used a chopstick to form *I love you*
From the tangle of floating letters.
I drank that sentence and began to glow.

Burrs & Thistles

What gifts do you bring me?
I see you walking
Across the baseball diamond,
A stick like a sword
Whacking at the tall grass.
The tips of your shoes
Will be green
As our love is green,
And your hair is the color
Of wheat. You see me,
And I wave.
You drop your stick
And run to me
Like Mercury,
Burrs, thistles, flakes
Of grass hooking
On your pant cuffs.

Later, at our favorite
Place at the river,
I'll whisper, "Do you love me?"
And think how other

Girls want to grab
You like those burrs
And thistles. Jealous,
I'll pluck every one of them
And flick them into the wind . . .

Facts of Life

The bee will touch the flower,
And the flower will not
Complain. The weight
Of the bee is like a teaspoon
Of honey, and its wings
Transparent as the boy in fifth period—
He likes me, a bee hovering
Above as we share a microscope.
Am I his flower? We almost touch shoulders
When we bend to look
At the slide. We laugh.
I'm then stung—he leaves
My side and hovers over
A hippie girl named Sunflower.
In spring, boys don't last.

I Saw What You Did

You plunged your giant hand
Into your pocket
For dimes and nickels.
Some pennies rolled
Into the server's hand
At McDonald's,
The one place we can afford.
I heard you stutter,
"Chocolate, no, I mean—strawberry,"
My favorite flavor.
With two straws, we left
To sit on a bench—
Two pigeons stared at us.
When we lowered our faces
Toward that rosy milk shake,
Our eyes locked on each other,
And as we bumped heads,
Both of us almost
Choked from giggling.

I saw what you did—
You pretended to drink
From the straw.

You let me have most
Of the milk shake.
That was nice.
You called me sweet,
Strawberry sweet.

Rough Hands

Lotion is a slippery essence
Applied on a winter day

When an icy wind sings through the bare trees.
But I prefer my hands rough.

This way, when I hold yours,
You won't slip away.

Stars

I was spooked by a possum, the crunch of leaves,
Something going *hoot, hoot* in a tree.
I jumped when a fish jumped in the creek—
How you laughed your beautiful laugh.
You were guiding me along that creek
And finally up a hill to view the stars
Set deep against the black, black sky.
You held my hand. You said,
"You're my star." Here, *I* laughed.
Was this some line? You kissed me,
Then said the stars were really dead
But their light was moving earthward
And influencing everything from the seas
To our love. Yes, you used the word *love*.
I pulled my hair back.
You pressed your body against mine.
No longer scared of possums, the rustling leaves,
Or the sounds in the trees,
I was happy there was something called stars.

Natural Talent

You brought out a can of chicken noodle soup
And set its contents in a pot
Over the stove's collar of blue flames.
"Wow," I said, "you can cook."
The refrigerator's bulb shone on your handsome face
When you brought out a block of cheese—
You deftly cut little squares
And placed them onto saltines.
"Where did you learn all this?" I asked,
And you shrugged your shoulders.
I even liked how you turned on the kitchen faucet
With your elbow—you had to keep
Your fingers clean—and whittled little pieces
Of salami. We ate looking at each other,
Me so obviously in love. I asked, "Do you iron?"
You nodded—god, you have shiny hair!
After we ate, you asked me to take . . .
To take off my blouse! "Slow down," I said,
Hands on my hips. Then I understood.
You gave me a sweatshirt to wear
While you sewed on my loose fourth button.
Where did you learn this,
Multitasking lover boy of mine?

Obsession

Three photos of you on the front of my binder,
Two inside when I flip it open.
Downloaded photos of you on my bedroom wall,
In a locket my cat paws jealously,
And in my diary I lock with a key.
I'm obsessed with you. This spring wherever
I turn I see you, even in the faces
Of cumulus clouds I could pinch like a cheek.
I had my eyes checked last week
And the optometrist with beady eyes said,
"A curious case. Young lady, there's a picture
Of a boy at the back of your retinas."

Don't You See

If only you would turn
And see me. I think I'm nice,

And you're nice, too.
Does that mean we're compatible?

And look! We go to the same
School, at the same hour,

And under the same sun.
The blossoms are fluttering

From the fruitless cherry tree.
But is *this* fruitless? I'm flying

In and out of your shadow,
Stepping up steps,

Down steps, slowing
For water at the drinking fountain,

And bending over to tie my shoe.

If only you would turn
And see me

Seeing you.

Signs

At the beginning of baseball season,
You spoke of the distance between like and love.
This made me bite my lower lip in worry.
I think you were telling me something—
Are you done with me? Is your life all baseball?
Or maybe there's another girl.
I've seen your eyes slide away from me
And look at others. Okay, I'm jealous.
Now, from the bleachers, I watch each thing
You do—touching your cap,
Digging dirt from your cleats—and think
You're telling me something,
Like the third-base coach
Touching his nose and mouth.

Is that a sign for you to run?

Strategy

I went to class, sat in a chair
That wobbled and rocked. Got up

And changed seats.
I got up again, and again.

That's how I happened
To sit next to you.

Exaggeration

I knew you were in love.
At the restaurant you raced to get the door,
And while the sign said PULL,
You pushed, the heels of your shoes
Losing traction. People gathered around us,
Confused, as you begged, "No, no, let me!"
But you pushed instead of pulled.
Sweat glistened on your upper lip
And your face—I can still see it—was red.
You stopped. You informed the crowd, "It's stuck."
When a little old lady stepped up to open the door,
Everyone rudely rushed in front of us—
We had to wait twenty minutes for a table.

Okay, I exaggerate. But not when I say
I knew you were in love with me,
And I with you, the boy pushing ahead in life.

Meaning What?

When I heard the phrase
I long for you,
I first thought it was bad grammar
And then began to think,
No, it's something like *long* book,
Long movie, *long* drive to look
At the mountains or the sea,
Or it's Dad examining
Every dinosaur bone and dinosaur egg
At the Natural History Museum—
Now that's long! But when I turned
Thirteen, I finally understood,
And so did my classmate Jennifer Lee,
Her pretty face red for Brandon.
I asked, "How do you say 'I long for you'
In Mandarin?" and she said, *"Wo xi huan ni."*
I really didn't understand what she was saying,
But now I know what she meant.

Consequence

When a stone bridge fails,
You can rebuild it with your hands.

With love, when it falls,
The rocks shoot sparks. Gossips

Gather at the river's edge,
Skipping stones across the water,

Asking intently, "Who brought it down?"

Full Price

We missed the half-price
Matinee. But that was okay.
We walked around and did math
In our heads, both of us poor
But geniuses for figures.
Then you helped a man
Push a car barely alive
On the fumes of precious gas.
When the man tried to press
Ten dollars into your palm,
You said, "No, sir, no, we're fine."

We returned to the theater
And looked up at the marquee—
The movie was called *Totally and Forever.*
You held my hand
As you would have in the theater,
And under the halo of lights
I explained the plot.

Jealousy

In the hallway, I pass your ex-girlfriend,
Tall as me, brown hair and eyes like me,

And have to think, *What's the difference?*
I think of her in your arms,

And the cute things you said into her ear.
What did you tell her? What secrets?

When I turn to spy on her, I see she also turned—
Tall as me, brown hair and eyes like me,

And both of us baring our teeth.

Black Books

Each time I get a boyfriend,
I buy a black book and promise myself
To take notes. He's nice,
He's not nice. He buys me a soda,
He takes it back and drinks it all!
His grilled teeth shine like a lie.
He turns his pockets inside out—
"I'm poor," he claims,
And *my* ten dollars flies from *my* hand
To his. "We need gas money," he says,
But why am I always on the sidewalk
Waving good-bye?
Will I ever find the right boy?

They say we must cut down
Trees to make paper. If so,
I'm guilty of cutting down a forest—
Little black books in my drawer,
And, like me, barely used.

Barriers

Who will understand us?
Not your parents or mine,
As I'm Japanese
And you're Mexican,
Both of us third generation.
What do we know—
Gracias, por favor,
Arigato, sayonara.
Who will understand us?
Holding hands,
I notice the color of
Our skin becoming one
In time.

Testing You

You said I smelled like a flower
And I gripped your arm.

"Okay, lover boy, what kind of flower?"
That stopped you. Your eyes

Searched around, baffled.
Nothing behind them but the NBA teams?

You answered, "A red flower."
And brat me said, "Oh, you mean a jasmine."

You nodded your bobble head.
"Yeah, that one. You smell hecka pretty."

That's okay. I knew you didn't know
The names of flowers. A jasmine is white,

And your face would be red
If I told you my father, a gardener,

Would make you shovel seven years
For my sweet-smelling hand, if you should ask.

The Big Chill

We have lost something.
In September your hand squeezed mine
And the next month we just walk next
To each other, shoulders touching,
You smiling but not really.
It's not the same. The sun rises, the sun falls.
Shadows the color of diesel exhaust
Roll across the lawn,
And the trees are unlatching their leaves.
It's not the same as when we first met.
It's November. After football practice,
You show me the bruises on your arms.
I wish I could show you the one spreading
Around my heart.
In December the snow will erase
Our footsteps. You'll be gone.
My chilled breath will hang in the air
And my lonely shadow will walk behind me.

First Kiss

I haven't been kissed,
But I'm waiting.

I'm a little scared. Do I hold my breath,
Close my eyes, and peek when he

Leans in to me? Do I lick my lips,
And offer my neck for the first one?

My fingernails are chewed from worry.
My cheeks are red as sin. Nothing has happened,

Nothing yet. But when it does, I'll call
My best friend and tell what took only seconds

For hours and hours.

Anonymous Tug

I swear the school clock is slow,
And our teacher is repeating himself every three minutes.
Poor Mr. Mathews has more hair on his ears
Than on his shiny head. He's a gentle
Scholar with chalk dust on his eyelashes
And lunch on the front of his shirt.
Can't the clock hurry up and do a quick lap?
Can't we have a fire drill?
I'm thinking of you, my secret pretty boy.
When the bell rings, I'm going to toss myself
Into the hallway. If you feel a tug
On your backpack, think of me,
A fish swimming upstream
In the river of bodies.

Paper Boat

You folded a piece of paper
Into a boat and set it on the pond.

We stepped back, hand in hand,
And watched your creation drift.

Then *they* arrived, two ducks
That began to peck at your little ship.

I covered my mouth with my hand,
Stomped my foot, and scolded, "Go away!"

The duck with cruel eyes lifted
Your paper boat into its bill—

Three pecks made it sink, just another
Piece of litter at the pond's edge.

We were young, not yet fourteen.
What chance could our love have

In a world so rough?

Fake Love

When you moved away,
You said you would write and call.

I checked my e-mail and my cell phone
A hundred times a day.

You were a fake. I was the one who helped
You in math. You didn't learn anything!

Like you are *one*, I am *two*, we're a *pair*!
You were a fake, an unsolved math problem,

Even when you put on a clip-on bow tie
And teased your hair to look like Einstein.

You were not smart enough to know
What you would lose.

The Invisible Girl

I'm unnoticed, some call me clumsy.
I wear a Band-Aid on my finger

Like a wedding band. Band-Aids
On my knees, near my ankles,

On my heart. I hurt a lot,
From the cruelty of boys.

I brush against them in the hallway.
In the cafeteria, they push in front

Of me and step on my shoes.
Still, I scribble hearts on my binder.

This is who I am: a girl taped
From head to toe. Pull off the Band-Aids,

I'll be the Invisible Girl,
Everyone passing through me,

No one touching.

Neighborhood

How long is a bus ride
Somewhere pretty,
With flowers in window boxes,
Green lawns and wind chimes?
Here, what do we know
But gangsta rap
Behind the smoked windows
Of long squeaky cars,
And the yellow grill on the face
Of a thug leaning from
The porch, calling, "Hey, baby."
I'll walk on by to the store
And when I return find his shadows
Crumpled on a dead lawn.

Love, how long is a bus ride
Somewhere pretty,
To some park where the gophers
Come up from their holes,
Not go down to take cover.

Horses

Call me this afternoon,
Call and say, "Hey."
I'll bare my teeth like a horse,
Say, "Hay's for horses,"
And whinny. It's something
We do. We're in love
And we play along
Like horses—carrots
And apples, a piece of sugar,
And to make you beautiful,
A comb for your mane!
Like a horse in a stall,
I'm waiting. Please call,
Love, and if you like,
You can name me Misty
Or Moonglow, any horsey name.
But first punch in my number,
You cowpoke! Be yourself,
And say, "Hey."

Playing Football

For a while I liked
Boys with curly hair,
And then straight hair,
Short Afros, or daring boys
With green spiky hair.

Now at the beginning
Of football season, I like
Them with cropped heads,
Like Michael, my hero next door!
Coach made him shave
His head, and made him
Do enough push-ups
That an empire of muscles
Dwells on his chest!
On my leaf-strewn lawn,
He plays catch with me.
But I drop them all, the long
And short spirals,
Even easy shovel passes.
To me, he's so cute.
If he were my boyfriend,
I wouldn't let him slip
From my hands.

Lazy Cupid

I first heard about Cupid
When I was nine, how this chubby
Little guy would pull back his arrow
And plug someone with love.
You could be at the supermarket
Bending down to pick up a case
Of Gatorade when Cupid,
A sneak by the rack
Of candy bars, would shoot
An arrow into your thigh—
Suddenly, in love,
Your taste was for a boy,
Or a girl—forget the Gatorade!

I'm thirteen, thirsty for the love
Of a boy at school,
But where is Cupid now?
Why is he a lazy
Couch potato? Is he cramming
A handful of chips
Into his mouth, a grubby
Little guy with food
Between his teeth?
I'm on the couch myself,

Sleepy from watching
A movie that's no good.
I rest my eyes. I close them
And see you, my would-be guy.
If only Cupid would get off the couch.

For the Love of Dogs

When you said you liked dogs
I introduced you to Roger, an Australian mix,
And the three of us—a love
Triangle—went to Dog Park.
Pooches exercise there.
They frolic, roll, slobber on balls, catch Frisbees.
Sometimes they bare their teeth and fight.
But not Roger, my pacifist dog.
No, he's the kind who'll shake paws
And politely wipe his nose
On the kerchief around his neck.
Love, I like how your hair is shaggy,
That your sweater, when wet, smells of dog.
And that you itch when I'm around.
I love you for this. Remember one day
At Dog Park, you and Roger
Were among other dogs,
All jumping around, fleas jumping from one
Pooch to another? I slapped my thighs
And called, "Come here, boy."
You looked up, and with the other dogs,
Came running!

Little Puppy

I can't get enough of you.
In biology I secretly flip open my cell
And look at you, digitally caught.
You're so cute, hair slanting over your left eye,
And a chain on your neck—
You are my little puppy.
If I attach a leash
And lead you around the city,
Would you snag a Frisbee with your teeth?
Would you eat from my hand?
My grandma says, "It's puppy love,"
An old phrase from her time.
I might agree.
You're my puppy, a nice puppy.
Your paws know their place,
Not like the dogs my girlfriends see,
Paws everywhere, and dirty, too!

Pears

The tears inside a pear are sweet,
And I like to think

Of us as pears,
Sweet and a little round.

The world is cruel.
When it bites us,

We cry sweet little tears.

Bossy Girl

I've forgotten everything you said to me,
Except one word: Good-bye.
It rings in my ears. You walked away,
Your left shoulder higher than the right,
And I wanted to shout, "Stand up straight!"
Even as you were leaving.
Now I cry in my bedroom.
My shoulders heave up and down.
I can't help the way I am,
Telling everyone what to do.
Even my goldfish, his ugly mouth
Pouting, makes me angry.
"Stop it!" I scold, and the goldfish turns away,
Swishing his tail at me.
Why should I care?
At least my shoulders are straight,
Not like yours,
As I cry alone.

When I Lost You

I wrote in my diary
All about you—first kiss,
Second kiss, a hug at the mall
With shoppers swinging
Their bags, envious
Of our young love?
Each time I wrote
I had to unlock the diary
With a little key. I wrote
In a rainbow of
Colors—pink of flowers,
Baby blue of sky, black
Of tornadoes, and gold
Of what we were worth.
Then the colors changed
When I lost you.
Now I'm the color of
A bruise,
And you're faded yellow,
The color of lies.

Time with You

We're thirteen, almost fourteen,
And so much in love

We want the years to pass—
Clouds roll at super speed, rains fall,

Flowers unfold and die at the snap
Of our fingers. I want to stuff sand

Through a fat hourglass,
And rip the pages from the calendar.

Let me blow candles from my cake.
Let my puppy stretch to full size.

When we turn eighteen,
Time will become a canoe on a still lake.

We'll be in that canoe, you with your
Guitar—one string busted. But who cares?

Let it be the same song,
Let the springtime flowers wave in the wind

But never let their petals fall.

Sparks

When I pull clean clothes
From the dryer—static
And sparks—I'm reminded
Of you at football practice,
Mud in your cleats,
Grass streaks, maybe blood.
I imagine your face flushed,
Grimacing as you throw
Your helmet into a tackle.
The result? Yellow
And red sparks,
Little devil horns of hurt.

Love, don't hurt yourself.
Come to me
When you're done,
And I'll put your jersey
Through the hot cycle. Rest
On the couch. Bring your face
To my face—sparks on
Our lips—and we'll clunk heads,
Gently, my love, gently.

Home Alone, and Liking It

My parents are gone, the television is off,
And I can flip open my phone
And kiss your image.
In my pajamas I dance around the living room.
I like being alone on Saturday,
I like having nothing to do. From the front window
I see it's partly cloudy. It may rain,
Or not rain. I may call you or not call,
My sleepy lover boy.
I'll pet my cat, ring the bell under its neck.
I'll dance around the living room some more,
Then into the kitchen (I'll nibble at toast),
And into the bathroom (I'll shower and sing).
It's Saturday, partly cloudy,
And I'm alone. You're a bear in bed,
And I'm a bird dancing in the living room
Singing off-key but singing anyway.
I can flip open my cell and look at you.
I'm home alone, so much in love.
I'm home alone, and liking it.

A Boy's Body,
His Words

Mirror

I walk to my bedroom mirror
And find you there, a reflection,
Some assembled light. I run my hands
Through my hair, and smile,
Then stop smiling. You're miles away,
On vacation at a lake that eats at the shore.
But let me believe, let me believe,
This afternoon hour
You're pulling the hair behind your ear
And stepping knee-deep in the lake,
And your baby brother, naked as Cupid,
Is shoving mud into a pail.
I see you skip a stone over the water,
See you march into the lake, chills on your arms.
You call me cute, but how long will you be mine?
My breath fogs the glass.
When I wipe it, you're gone.

The Second Button

The button hangs, as if it's done something wrong,
And what have we done wrong
But hold hands in the parking lot?
When your mother honked
We jumped,
And our hands jumped like fish.
You lifted your backpack, the weight of history
And algebra, and hurried to her,
The threads of your pants frayed, dragging little pieces
Of string. All the way home,
My head hung down,
Like the button on a thread.

Open House

When Mom said, "Come with me,"
I sighed and thought, *Not again.*
On Sunday afternoons
Mom likes to see how others live,
Their furniture and kitchens,
And, I, a good son, get into the car.

I'm glad I did—
A girl with her mother
Walked down the steps
As we climbed up.
We passed,
And I could see her
See me. There were roses
In the flower bed,
Stocks and freesia.
But she was a different kind of flower,
With pink buds beneath her blouse.

Vegan for Your Love

No chicken or chops,
No burgers or chow mein with pork,

No milk shakes thick as wet cement,
No buttered bread or my favorite beef jerky.

"I'm hardly hungry at all," I say,
And smooth the blanket where we lay in nature,

Ants with their antennae up and feeling
For handouts. I've lost four pounds

In two weeks, and by the end of the month,
I'm going to be like that red ant—

Waist so thin, I'm a vegan begging
For sprouts and, oh please, a single blade of grass.

A Long Weekend Without You

The wind blows west,
Hauling clouds in the spring weather.

I lie on a recliner in the yard
And wait for your face to take shape

Among those clouds. There, now I see you:
Nose and forehead,

The chin I once touched
And made myself shiver.

Love is like weather, cold or hot,
Nothing between. I watch

The clouds, the shadows like
A warning. I touch my face.

Is it rain from you, or a tear
From inside me?

So Much Alike

If only we hadn't moved away,
I would still know you,
Girl in the third row,
Your blouse buttoned all the way up.
I liked you. Didn't you know?
Because of you I wore a shirt with buttons,
Polished my shoes, and combed my hair,
Even went to church because I heard you did.
I almost cried
On that field trip to the aquarium
When I saw two penguins
With their little wings touching.
They had each other
And now I have no one, just arms at my sides,
Now and then flapping,
Now what, now what?

Fall Dance

When I promised to take you
To the fall dance,
You rose on tiptoes
To kiss me on the chin.
You cooed, "We'll waltz."
I smiled, swallowed,
And kicked through leaves,
Worried. What was
A waltz? I learned when
My mom swept me
Through the living room,
Her hand in my hand,
My other on her waist.
When the phone rang,
She handed me a
Broom, and said, "Practice."

So I held the thinnest girl ever,
My flat-chested partner,
And swished and swayed,

Dipped and bowed.
On the night of
The fall dance, Mom used
That broom to sweep me
From the house.

Country Music

I wish I could write you the saddest country song
About loneliness, horses, a pretty girl

Broken up by failed love. But what would I do with it?
I can't sing, or play guitar.

I love you so much. A melody runs through
My mind, but I'm not sure if it's mine.

Country music makes you sad.
I'm going to put on my granddad's cowboy hat,

And lick a pencil and write a song on an envelope.
But first I'm going to eat a peach

And think of you as a peach, something really sweet.
I'm going to get my dog to howl as I write,

There was this pretty girl, hanging tears on a line . . .

Beautiful Trouble

They say you have a tattoo of a butterfly
On your thigh, but how will I know?
That you can uncurl cigarette smoke at will,
That you can cuss in six languages,
That your last boyfriend is using a whole box
Of Kleenex to wipe away his river of tears.
These are rumors, just rumors.
But I can see. You're dressed in beautiful trouble,
The skirt that swings and the low-cut blouse,
And I may as well mention the red smile,
The ring on your loveliest toe,
And the glance in a compact mirror,
Seeing me watch you.
When you raise your hand in class,
Your bracelets ring. You seldom get the answer
Right, but who cares!
My dad, a deacon in the church, warns,
"Watch out for girls who cause trouble."
Indeed, I watch every day as you swing
Down the hallways, the little roll of muscle
In your calf, and somewhere up higher,
The rumor of a butterfly.

Busted

What was it, three weeks ago?
I went to your house
And there, in the living room,
A robot vacuum cleaner
Whirled away, searching for dirt.
The noisy gadget was working around
The fireplace, choking on cinders,
Ashes, and burnt matchsticks.
Then it turned to me
And started sucking at my shoelaces.
Was it pulling away my dirt?
I had to grin. Only then
I sat you on the couch
And told you, "Yeah, I *had* a girlfriend
But we're over." But I was busted.
The robot vacuum cleaner,
Sensing a filthy lie—I hadn't
Yet *really* broken up with my girlfriend—
Chased me from your super-clean house.

Tree Bark

In front of campus we meet
And you whisper, "Dad doesn't like you."

I push my fingers underneath the bark,
Peel it like a scab. Does the tree hurt?

Does the sunlight press its warmth into the skin?
Does an ant visit this pain?

I push my fingernails into my skin,
And the bite hurts. What sun will heal me?

Simple Me

For you, beauty is natural,
Even as you push away from the cafeteria table
And carry your plate to the conveyor belt.
I hurry behind you, wobbly as the chair
You pushed away, and look at your plate.
I see that you left a few peas,
Those plump little guys jumping on the plate,
Almost doing a samba. I watch the plate
Disappear behind a curtain and think,
Lucky fork touched your lips.

A Certain Weakness

I'm 6'1", weigh 180, mostly muscle,
And hero of a 43–42 overtime game last week.

Did you see it? I scored the last basket
And was thrown into the air—and caught!

I rode to the locker room on the roar
Of victory. I'm strong, you see.

But if you were to bump into me in the cafeteria,
You, who are 5'3", slight as a swan,

My legs would buckle.
My friends would have to carry me away.

It's exhausting thinking of you,
And in this game of love, I don't think I can score.

The Koi at the Museum Pond

A large golden koi surfaced,
Wise as an old man with a Fu Manchu beard.

I thought, *He's going to tell me something,*
Something about us.

He lowered his head,
And a ripple spread on the greenish water.

I stared at the water reflecting the rolling clouds.
The day will pass, a week,

A month . . . I told myself that if I stir
The surface with the tip of my shoe

The ancient and wise koi will surface,
Even larger. When he opens his mouth,

He'll speak our names.

The Birds and the Bees

First Dad hitched
Up his pants, unbuckled

His belt because dinner
Was spaghetti, and lowered

Himself into his recliner.
He ran his hand over

His face, then looked at
His fingernails—spaghetti sauce.

"Let me tell you about girls,"
Dad began, and then said,

"Well, they're usually shorter
Than us guys." I was thinking

Of Sarah from biology,
How she came up

To my shoulder,
And the scalpel in her hand—

The poor frog didn't blink
When she ran a slice

Up its belly.
He then said, "They cry

Sometimes, and they like shoes."
Where was Dad going?

"Girls are smarter," he added,
"But we sort of know

More practical things"—
He pointed to the

Ceiling and I knew what
He meant—the cooler on the roof

I oiled last weekend.
"Girls are emotional," he started,

But then leveled his gaze
On the television.

"What the heck!"
Dad crowed. "It's snowy."

I had to climb to
The roof to get the picture

Right for him, Dad
Yelling, "Left, turn it left,

No right, right I said!"
I never learned about

The birds and the bees
Until later.

Boy Artist

I think of you miles away.
We're on vacation, surf and sun,

And campfires under icy stars.
You're lovely. I draw hearts in the sand,

And the wind nudges them away.
That's okay. It's practice.

With the beach as my canvas, I draw hearts,
And the tide at four in the afternoon

Laps at the edges, dissolves our initials.
But our love will never wash away.

I'll be back in two days,
Sand under my fingernails,

Some in my ears from laying my head
On the beach and thinking of you.

Rumors

They say love makes you speechless,
That it takes your breath away,

And right now, as you round
The corner in the hallway,

I, who was telling a friend about the F chord
On a guitar, become speechless.

You pass, and I double over,
Like when, in first grade, Marc Steinberg

Hit me in the stomach
And took my breath away.

But this strike, this beauty of yours,
Is another kind of hurt.

Faces

With a pen, I drew little faces
On your fingertips, ten in all,
And you said, "You love me, huh?"
They were happy faces.
You showed them to your
Friend, who laughed,
Clapped, and said,
"Wow, you're so lucky, girl."

That was between third
And fourth period,
And by fifth period—
I don't know how
This happened—I fell
In love with this other
Girl, a musician who
Plays first violin in orchestra.

You and I met after school.
I kicked leaves, bit
My upper and lower lip
A hundred times,
And then confessed,

"You know Rebecca . . ."
You made a face, cried.
You raised your hands
And wiggled the fingertips
At me—the ink had run.
Each little face
Was sobbing, dropping
Little black tears.

Rationale

Already tall at thirteen, she walks
In platform shoes. I can't help

But think like a guy.
We could use a center—

We're 0–3 at the start of the season,
And so ugly on the court

We could use beauty.

A Lesson for Us

I rode over on my bike
And you hopped onto the bar,
Giggled when I took the grassy hill
Down your lawn to the park.
We lay on the grass,
Half in, half out of shadows
And smiled sleepily at the sky.
I kissed your knuckles
And you kissed me
Near my mouth,
Then on my mouth.
We then watched a couple
From a wedding party
Pushing a car. "See," I said,
"See how much love costs?"
The flowers in the woman's hair
Scattered like confetti
And with each push from
The back fender,
Anger sparked
From her knife-sharp heels.

Eternal Love

What's the meaning of time?
You said, "I'll be with you forever."

We lasted two weeks, one afternoon,
A half hour, a few minutes,

A sweep of seconds on the last day
Of the solstice. This sorrow

You gave me remains.
I could paw at the calendar of hurt,

And you'll be there
Like radium, like uranium,

Whatever element lasts forever.
But who cares about me?

Some joker said, "Love is eternal
As long as it lasts."

I feel him.

Danger

The storm dropped six feet of snow,
And with it, an electrical wire in front of our house.

It snaps and moves like a snake.
When will the police arrive?

Or a worker who will set safety cones in the road?
Isn't it a hazard, a hot wire in snow?

School is closed. The house is dark.
I'm thinking of you huddled near a candle.

If I knew you were in trouble,
I would take a shovel and shovel my way

To your house, six blocks away,
And risk live wires hissing like snakes.

Love, I know, can be hazardous to my health.

Time

Tired of the same cats in the Dumpster,
Tired of blaring radios, of gangsters with their grills,

We rode one bike to the park,
Where we bought a single bottle of water

And lay on the spongy grass. I told you
Three times that I loved you,

And you said, "Okay, write it on my shoulder."
You showed me your pinkish shoulder,

And I wrote, *Luv you, Madison.* It was then
I understood we are flesh and blood,

And, like all others, we will die in time.
We lay on the grass, not touching,

Just facing the immense sky. Clouds rolled
And migrating ducks, dark as commas,

Were flying south. I closed my eyes.
I took your hand in mine and imagined us dead,

With the world wheeling above us
But you at my side, Madison, you and I touching

For all of time.

Pomegranate as My Heart

I don't have much to offer
But this pomegranate,
A fruit ancient as the Nile,
A fruit that bleeds like a heart.
I can only think of how beautiful you are.

If I could crack open this pomegranate
And share it with you,
Would that be a nice gift?
We could nibble these jewels,
Smile red smiles.

I wait at the curb, tossing the pomegranate
From one hand to the other.
Come out, please. I'm waiting.
How many times will I juggle
This ancient fruit before it drops?
If I do—and it splits open
To reveal its jewels—
I'll give you the largest part.

Driftwood

When she said no,
I took my loneliness to the river,

Frozen only a month ago.
Sunlight lit the first blossoms of spring

And made early March appear beautiful.
But it wasn't for me.

I stared at the slow cargo of blossoms,
And the ripples that hurried them along.

I kicked sand that sprayed like salt,
And sighed a dozen times.

I noticed driftwood that resembled arms
And legs. That's how I felt,

Lifeless, in other words.
You may laugh, but I bent over the river,

Adding to that ancient flow,
A young man's sadness when a girl says no.

Getting to Know You

It was rude of me to bend down
And read what it said on your ankle,

But it was unkind
Of you to walk away.

I had to follow like a duck,
Until you stopped—you placed

Your shoe on my thigh.
I retied your loose shoelaces,

And got to read the name
On your ankle bracelet—Jenny.

That was the first time we touched—
Your shoe on my thigh,

And your little toes,
Wiggling behind the cloth

Of worn tennis shoes.
It was so cute—the little toe

Was peeking out,
Peeking at me!

Imagination

To travel, we can use our imagination,
Or so says Mr. Fried, our English teacher.
If we just picked up a book,
We could be in France, Brazil, or Norway.
Mr. Fried, you're a nice man,
But, please, *you* pick up the book
And float on an iceberg to Norway!
You swat mosquitoes in hot, hot Brazil.
After school, I'm rolling
My skateboard thirty-three blocks,
Sixteen of which I'll be terrorized
By pit bulls and thugs lurking
Like vultures on car fenders.
You see, I have a girl
On the other side of town.
I don't want to read
About love, but feel love—
Her hand in mine,
Her hair against my throat,
And the pink bud of her tongue . . .

She's shy as a pony and just as tall.
Mr. Fried, you're a nice man,
A smart man. I'm sure if I told you
About my girl and me,
You could write a book.

A View of Heaven

Love, come to my house
And we'll climb my roof—
I read on the Internet
The moon will rise at 7:28
Over a forest of TV antennas
And the trees rustling their confetti
Of heart-shaped leaves.
Let the neighbors watch
What they watch. But let us, my love,
Watch the moon lift the stars.
Don't we know our planets?
We could count them out,
One by one, and admit to ourselves
That Venus is our favorite.
The planet of love?

I may be wrong.
But I'm not wrong about you,
And that the moon will not wait—
It rises at 7:28, and if you
Arrive before then
I will take your hand and lead you up
The ladder, you a star,
My Venus rising.

Forest of Boulders

Out of love,
I'm going to walk

Into the forest
And sit next to

A gray boulder.
Rain will fall,

Thickets grow
Around my feet

Until after
So many years

I will blend into
That boulder.

Then another boy
My age, hurt

In the heart,
Will hunker next to me.

Rain will fall,
Hawks settle

On his hardening
Shoulders

Until he, too,
Becomes a boulder.

Time passes.
Shooting stars cut across

The sky. The president declares
It a national park.

Hikers will climb
Over and step

Around these boulders
In the forest, where boys go

When a girl says no.

Leaving the Bookstore

Through the glass door greasy with fingerprints,
I couldn't help it. My eyes slid

From you to a girl in a red halter,
Tight jeans, sandals, straight blond hair,

Freckles on her shoulders, a toe ring . . .
I was taking inventory of her beauty,

And you caught me. I asked lamely,
"Does she go to our school?"

You narrowed your eyes at me,
Flashed red coals from deep inside you,

Wherever you keep your anger.
We walked in silence to the next store,

Me, a little dog, a few steps behind.

Love Medicine

From then on he couldn't sleep.
And if his stepmother
Made him his favorite meat loaf,
He propped his chin
On his hand and thought,
Just one bite—I'm not really hungry.
He couldn't do his homework.
He couldn't do his chores.

When a friend called
And said, "Hey, man, let's lift weights,"
He moaned that he was sick.
He was lovesick.
He couldn't get this girl
Out of his mind.

He wished that he could go
To the pharmacy and stagger down
An aisle to find Love Medicine—
In liquid and tablet forms
And, perhaps, Band-Aids to apply
To his heart, for he hurt there
And other places.

He would examine boxes
And read the instructions,
"Take every hour. If symptoms worsen
Discontinue use and consult your doctor."
If only there was
Medicine to correct his dizziness
Over this girl in algebra.
But she was the medicine, a remedy.
She was the doctor pressing
A cool hand to his forehead
And cooing, "There, there. All better."

Spreading Love

My girlfriend was bouncing down
The hallway, so happy, so full of love,
And her hair lifting beautifully
After each bouncy step.

She was carrying the roses I gave her,
Petals unhooking and dropping to the ground.
She hugged me, smiled, and said, "Hi, ugly."
This was how much we loved each other.

Later, when I walked around campus,
I saw petals everywhere,
My girlfriend so busy showing her friends
The flowers I bought her.

I had to smile. She was in love with me,
And those poor roses, just stems at the end
Of the day, blew across the schoolyard
Like kisses.

Mystery

She showed me the scar on her wrist
And said, "It doesn't hurt
Anymore." I swallowed my fear
And asked how she got it.

She pulled her hair behind
Her ears and whispered, "An accident."
That was it, no more.
It was after school. We were playing
Volleyball in cold weather.
Our breath hung in the air
And our wrists stung
When we slugged the ball.

I couldn't get it out of my mind.
The scar was shaped like a smile—
But I knew it was nothing
To laugh about.

Hard Work

I'm exhausted from being in love—
My fingers are blistered from writing

You e-mail love letters.
I hurt from carrying a huge torch in my heart.

No one told me love would be such hard work.
Every day I put on clean clothes, floss my teeth,

And breathe on mirrors to check my breath.
And for our first-month anniversary

I memorized a poem and worked three hours
In my neighbor's yard—with the money earned

I bought you flowers that I held before you,
All the while reciting a Sylvia Plath poem.

I have my doubts now.
I've lost weight and my lips are chapped

From saying how much I love you.
I have rings under my eyes

And my bottle of cologne is half-empty.
I'm a little more than half-empty.

My ride, as you know, is a bicycle.
Next time, when we're going somewhere,

Could I sit on the bar and you pedal?
I'm exhausted from being in love.

Iowa Evening

A shooting star burns across the sky,
And I make a wish

On its brief earthly descent.
I wish you were here

Next to me on this tractor in the field.
I helped Dad from a little

Before sunup, dropped coins
Of sweat in the cornfields,

And then washed the car—
Mom had some church thing

To do and Dad went along.
Alone, in my aching bones,

I ate dinner and then went outside
To feel the evening wind.

You're on my mind. I think of you,
The city girl, and whether

You really love me. At the sight
Of another shooting star,

I wish you would suddenly
Appear from the tall stalks

Of corn, a blanket on your arm.
I watch the stalks, a breath

Of evening wind rustling the leaves.
I wait nearly an hour

At the wheel of a tractor,
Tired as a horse.

The shooting stars fall
All over the county

And boys like me, seated
On tractors, truck fenders, porches,

Are wishing on stars—
I'm hoping that somewhere,

Perhaps at our place,
A certain girl will part

The tall stalks of corn
And throw a blanket

Into the air. Where it spreads
Is where this girl will lie

With her country boy.

Playing Our Parts

If you love me,
Meet me in front of the theater,
Where the movie
Is *Hug Me If You Mean It*.
Let's not go in.
Just meet me there,
And we'll play the parts
In that movie we'll never see.
I'll be the boy, you the girl,
And the world—traffic and cars
Hurling through red lights—
Our backdrop. We'll play our
Parts for free. I'll kiss you,
And the director inside me will shout,
"Cut—hug and let's do it again."
There will be stars in my eyes,
Stars in yours. I like perfection.
I'll do it until I get it right.

Out in Nature

Not much of a hill
As hills go—and it looks like

Ants are trying to claim it
And haul its leaves underground.

How do they do this? Only nature knows.
We step back to give them room.

Thousands of ants are everywhere,
With bits of lumber in their jaws.

You and I watch them
And their marvelous capacity for work.

Then we go in search
Of another hill where we can spread

A quilt. I want to lie at your side
And pluck your hair like a harp.

I know there's music inside you,
A song, some lyrics that speak my name.

It's my nature to love you.
You are beauty—flower, leaf, sunshine.

Let the ants have every small hill
But this one. We'll lie on the quilt

And listen to the wind with its rumors
Of love and longing.

Though I get tongue-tied,
Let love now speak our names.

An Act of Kindness

As an act of kindness I steer the mower
Around bees on our lawn.
Today, I don't want to hurt anyone,
And least of all, those making honey.

My stepfather watches from the porch.
He points and says over the noise,
"Buddy, you missed over there."

I'll go back,
But first I'll let the bees move
To another part of the lawn,
Or move to the flowering geranium.

I stop my mower, wipe my face.
I notice the kindness of bees.
They each drink from a flower
And let the next bee drink.
There's no shoving like students
In school, all of us at the fountain,
Wetting our lips, for we have a lot to say.

I'm thinking of you, love,
And the blades that may cut us down.
The world is cruel. People have knives,
And even their teeth look like knives.

What we could learn from the bees.